YEAR 5

Classwor'

Non-fic ion Texts

Eileen Jones

Published in 2004 by:
Nelson Thornes Ltd
Delta Place
27 Bath Road
CHELTENHAM
GL53 7TH
United Kingdom

04 05 06 07 08 / 10 9 8 7 6 5 4 3 2 1

A catalogue record for this book is available from the British Library

ISBN 0-7487-8657-0

Illustrations by Mike Phillips and Nick Schon
Page make-up by GreenGate Publishing Services

Printed in Great Britain by Ashford Colour Press

Acknowledgements
All texts written by Eileen Jones except:

'To save a file' reproduced by permission of Microsoft Corporation; 'How does the human respiratory system function', 'How do people breathe', and 'How is sound made' reproduced from *The Internet-Linked Book of Knowledge* by permission of Usborne Publishing 83–85 Saffron Hill, London EC1N 8RT, UK. Copyright © 2003 Usborne Publishing Ltd; 'Family life in Victorian Britain', 'Family gatherings', 'Family outings' and 'Children' taken from *Family Life in Victorian Britain* by Richard Wood. Reproduced by permission of Hodder and Stoughton Limited. Copyright © Richard Wood 1994; 'Index', 'Philosophers and scientists' and 'Arts and crafts' by Robert Nicholson are reprinted from *Great Civilisations* with the permission of Two-Can Publishing, an imprint of Creative Publishing International, Inc. Text copyright © Two-Can Publishing; Extract from the Warwick Castle website used by kind permission of Warwick Castle; Extract about Elsecar Heritage Centre taken from www.barnsley.co.uk in association with Elsecar Heritage Centre, Wath Road, Elsecar, Barnsley, S74 8HJ; Extract from The Bank of England website copyright © The Bank of England Museum; Extract from Lochwinnoch website copyright © RSPB 2004; Extract from Edinburgh Butterfly and Insect World website; 'He's everybody's Darling now' extract taken from *The Leamington Courier* December 19th 2003 Copyright © The Leamington Courier 2003.

Photographs: Text 1: Volcanic eruption – Photodisc 31 (NT); Text 2: Pompeii – Corel 684 (NT); Text 24: Young people looking at puppet show (BE041166 RM) copyright © Bettman/CORBIS; Text 28: Greek Urn – Corel 273 (NT), Zeus – Corel 473 (NT), Parthenon, Greece – Corel 397 (NT); Text 33: Countryside/England – Peter Adams/Digital Vision BP (NT), Fox/Britain – NatPhotos/Digital Vision AF (NT); Text 34 People/Elections – Photodisc 16 (NT) and Photodisc 33 (NT).

Cover image: DV6.028032 Digital Vision 6 (NT)

Every effort has been made to trace the copyright holders but if any have been inadvertently overlooked, the publishers will be pleased to make the necessary arrangement at the first opportunity.

Contents

How to use this book

What this book contains

- Extracts from published works, plus tailor-made extracts, all arranged and chosen specifically to match the examples of medium-term planning provided by the National Literacy Strategy
- Teaching ideas for each extract to get you started, covering some of the relevant text, sentence or word level objectives from the relevant unit

How you can use *Classworks Literacy Texts* with other resources

- The blocked unit structure means you can dip into the book to find resources perfect for what you're teaching this week – it doesn't matter what plan, scheme or other resource you're using
- There are two *Classworks Literacy Texts* books for every year from Reception (or Primary 1) to Year 6 (or Primary 7): one contains Fiction and Poetry, the other contains Non-fiction. Both books together contain texts for every unit of the medium-term plans

What each page does

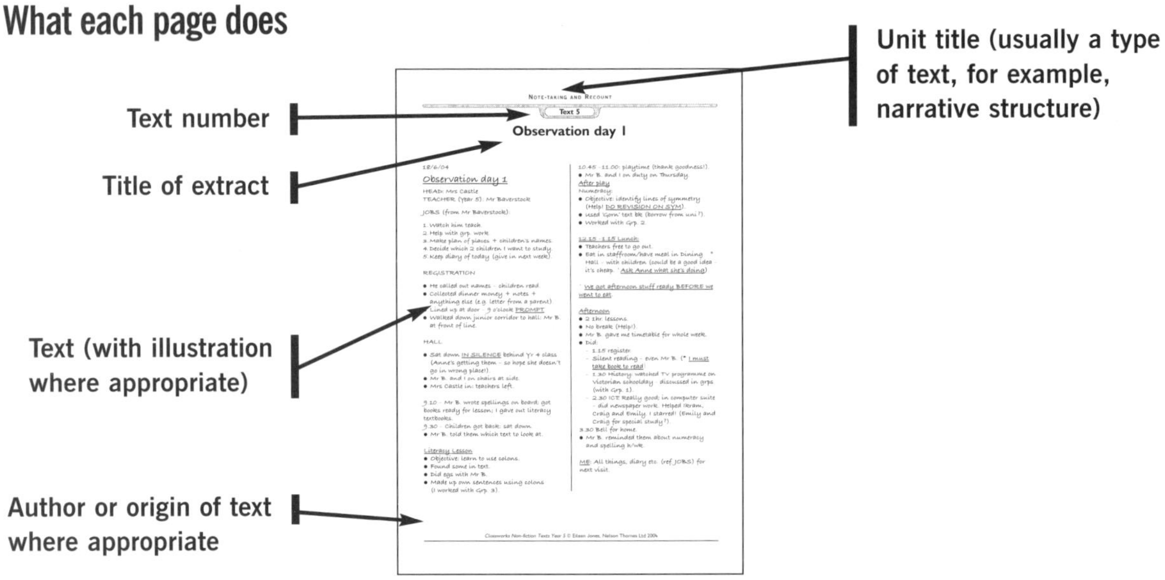

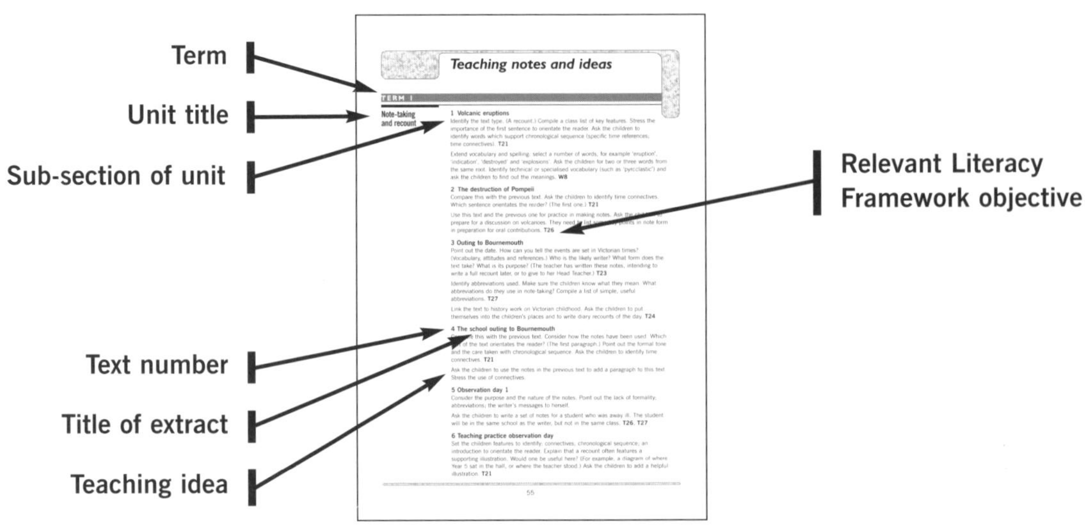

Text 1

Volcanic eruptions

In the 1990s, Montserrat, a small part of the Leeward Islands off the West Indies, suffered major volcanic activity.

However, the eruption was not a single affair. The island had experienced problems over a period of time. In July 1995, people living in the south of the island complained of a sulphurous smell: it was traced to the Chances Peak volcano. The volcano had given no trouble for 400 years, but this smell was an indication of renewed life.

Later in that same month, there were small earthquakes, steam explosions, and tephra falls. Experts recorded growth in the stem of the volcano, and veins began to split open on one side. There was every indication of an imminent eruption.

As a result, it was decided to evacuate the area, and in August 1995, over 6 000 people moved to the north of the island. The evacuation was only just in time: on 21 August, there was a volcanic eruption. The capital city of Plymouth, in the south-west of Montserrat, experienced 30 minutes of darkness, as ash and dust rained down. For the next eight months, a number of minor eruptions occurred, mainly involving the movement of ash.

The following spring, the situation worsened. Eruptions grew stronger. In April, there were instances of ash, rock, and gas – at very hot temperatures – being thrown into the air at heights up to 12 km, before creating a pyroclastic flow down the mountain. Again local areas were declared unsafe, and evacuation was ordered.

The volcano became quiescent, but in January 1997, enough grit and ash was forced upwards to result in most of the island being affected. There was considerable damage, and dangerously fast pyroclastic flows swept down the volcano's sides.

A few months later, on 25 June, the dome of the volcano caved in. Ash formed a nine km vertical cloud, blocking all sunlight for about 20 minutes. The resulting pyroclastic flows involved an area of four km square.

On 27 June, the first resulting deaths were reported, when it was decided that four missing people must have been buried by falling stones. Two months later, further movements resulted in ash and dust falls and pyroclastic flows: Plymouth, Montserrat's capital city, was destroyed. Then, for the rest of 1997 and on into 1998, regular, minor volcanic activity was reported.

The final eruption was on 13 January 1999, when an ash plume six km high was forced upwards, and an avalanche of hot gases and rocks swept down the eastern slopes of Chances Peak.

Adapted from 'Volcanoes' by Vincent Bunce

Text 2

The destruction of Pompeii

The destruction of Pompeii was brought about by natural disasters. Before the first of these disasters, the Roman city of Pompeii was a popular, thriving and bustling port.

The first disaster occurred in AD 63, when the area close to Naples in Italy suffered an earthquake. Pompeii, situated in that area, sustained considerable damage and much of the city was destroyed.

After that disaster, a period of building and reconstruction followed, resulting in a city prized by the Romans. Although the city was sited in the shadow of Vesuvius, a volcano, it was believed to be in no danger, for no further eruptions were predicted.

Then in AD 79, the second disaster occurred. People's predictions were shown to be wrong: the volcano began to erupt. At first there was the noise: the ominous rumbles. Then there was movement as the ground beneath people's feet shook. When the people of Pompeii looked above them, they were met by the terrifying sight of a mountain throwing out flames and dense black smoke.

From then on, the city darkened as the black cloud grew larger. People soon lost their distinction between night and day, and were left in a state of terrified panic and confusion. The volcano spurted out a crushing, burning mass of lava, stones and ash.

Panic came quickly to the city, as the inhabitants tried to make their escape. However, the efforts of many were thwarted by the confusing darkness and the intense heat. In the midst of all this, came a terrible rainstorm.

There followed three days of horrific conditions: repeated eruptions; thick smoke; poisonous gases; red-hot lava; ash; and finally, mud. The rain's deluge mixed with the lava and ash to form a growing mass of mud. Gradually, this monster began its descent down the mountain. As the mud began to slide, it gained in speed, strength and size. When it reached Pompeii, it consumed the city.

At the end of three days, the city, with its splendid buildings, its homes, and its thousands of inhabitants, lay buried. Pompeii had been destroyed.

Text 3

Outing to Bournemouth

Thursday, June 18th 1861

Outing to Bournemouth

7.30 a.m. Assembled on hill.
Register called: 47 – Jane Ellis missing.
Walked to station.
7.40 a.m. Station. Correct re-count.
7.45 a.m. Joined by Jane Ellis – Mother's excuse accepted.
Waited on platform; silent order.
7.50 a.m. Boarded the train.
Number checked.

Main places journeyed through

- Bishopstoke
- Southampton West
- Ringwood
- New Forest – delightful scenery

Conduct on journey

Controlled behaviour & quiet talking.
No eating or drinking (sweets confiscated from Jane Ellis).

Incidents on journey

2 cases of sickness: Jane Ellis & Thomas Croft.

Arrival

10.00 a.m. Arrived Bournemouth.
Alighted.
Roll call.
Proceeded to beach – via East Cliff Rd.

10.30 a.m. Arrived beach.
Roll call.
Permitted removal of heavy outerwear.
Refreshment.
Beach games (suitable decorum).

12 noon. Lunch – below promenade.

1.00 p.m. Walked ➡ pier.
1.30 p.m. Arrived pier.
Roll call: Jane Ellis missing.
1.35 p.m. Re-joined by distraught Jane Ellis – had fallen behind during walk.

1.30 – 3.30 p.m. Pier amusements – constant vigilance re. Jane Ellis.
Use of appropriate penny slot machines.
3.35 p.m. Roll call.
3.35 – 4.00 p.m. Made way via Overcliff to town gardens.
4.00 p.m. Roll call
V. enjoyable tea, kindly supplied by Bourn. Council.

4.30 – 6.00 p.m. Town band in gardens.

6.00 p.m. Proceeded ➡ Bournemouth Railway Station.
6.20 p.m. Delayed by fall by Jane Ellis – knee dressed at first aid hut.
6.30 p.m. Arrived station.
Roll call.
Awaited train – gd. order.
6.45 p.m. Boarded train.
6.50 p.m. Departure.

Train journey

Most children slept.
Repeat sickness incidents: Jane Ellis & Thomas Croft.

9.00 p.m. Arrived Basingstoke.
Alighted.
Roll call.
Collection by parents.

9.10 p.m. Final collection (Jane Ellis) – excuse given by mother.

Text 4

The school outing to Bournemouth

On Thursday June 18th 1861, a wonderful outing to Bournemouth was made. It was possible only because of the generosity and benevolence of Basingstoke Council, and the staff and scholars of the school are most grateful.

The day began with the assembly of the teacher and children at 7.30 a.m. on Hill Approach, Miss Steines having charge of a party of 48 children. First she proceeded to take her party on foot to the railway station, to await the 7.50 a.m. train to the seaside. Then she maintained good order at the station, before boarding the train and departing punctually.

After leaving Basingstoke, the train passed through places of note and interest, in particular Bishopstoke, then Southampton West and Ringwood. The party also had the pleasure of passing through the pleasing scenery of the New Forest.

During the journey, the children were well-behaved and their teacher had few incidents to recount. However, sweets had to be removed from one girl, and that same child, along with another, experienced sickness.

The next town after Ringwood was the renowned seaside town of Bournemouth, where the children and their teacher alighted at 10.00 a.m. From the station, it was a mere half hour before the party enjoyed beach refreshment and amusement. At each stage, Miss Steines was punctilious in her checking for the presence and decorous behaviour of each of her charges.

At noon, they partook of lunch in the shade below the promenade, whence they walked, an hour later, to the newly-constructed pier. Amusements for the children were carefully selected and supervised by their teacher, who continued to exercise great vigilance.

After a walk along Overcliff to Bournemouth's wonderful floral displays in its town gardens, tea was provided most generously by Bournemouth Town Council and was enjoyed gratefully by all. Then the fortunate party was entertained in the splendid gardens by delightful music from the town's celebrated band.

At 6 o'clock, the children and their teacher proceeded to the railway station, from whence they departed on the 6.50 p.m. train. Most children slept gratefully on their return journey, although sickness was repeated by the same two unfortunate children as earlier in the day.

When the train reached Basingstoke at 9.00 p.m. parents were waiting to collect their children, and by 9.10 p.m. the final child was returned safely to her parent.

Text 5

Observation day 1

18/6/04

Observation day 1

HEAD: Mrs Castle
TEACHER (Year 5): Mr Baverstock

JOBS (from Mr Baverstock):

1. Watch him teach.
2. Help with grp. work.
3. Make plan of places + children's names.
4. Decide which 2 children I want to study.
5. Keep diary of today (give in next week).

REGISTRATION

- He called out names – children read.
- Collected dinner money + notes + anything else (e.g. letter from a parent).
- Lined up at door – 9 o'clock PROMPT.
- Walked down junior corridor to hall: Mr B. at front of line.

HALL

- Sat down IN SILENCE behind Yr 4 class (Anne's getting them – so hope she doesn't go in wrong place!).
- Mr B. and I on chairs at side.
- Mrs Castle in: teachers left.

9.10 – Mr B. wrote spellings on board; got books ready for lesson; I gave out literacy textbooks.
9.30 – Children got back: sat down.
- Mr B. told them which text to look at.

Literacy Lesson
- Objective: learn to use colons.
- Found some in text.
- Did egs with Mr B.
- Made up own sentences using colons (I worked with Grp. 3).

10.45 –11.00: playtime (thank goodness!).
- Mr B. and I on duty on Thursday.

After play
Numeracy:
- Objective: identify lines of symmetry (Help! DO REVISION ON SYM).
- Used 'Gorn' text bk (borrow from uni?).
- Worked with Grp. 2.

12.15 –1.15 Lunch:
- Teachers free to go out.
- Eat in staffroom/have meal in Dining Hall – with children (could be a good idea – it's cheap. *Ask Anne what she's doing).

* We got afternoon stuff ready BEFORE we went to eat.

Afternoon
- 2 1hr. lessons.
- No break (Help!).
- Mr B. gave me timetable for whole week.
- Did:
  - 1.15 register.
  - Silent reading – even Mr B. (* I must take book to read).
  - 1.30 History: watched TV programme on Victorian schoolday - discussed in grps (with Grp. 1).
  - 2.30 ICT: Really good; in computer suite – did newspaper work. Helped Ikram, Craig and Emily. I starred! (Emily and Craig for special study?).

3.30 Bell for home.
- Mr B. reminded them about numeracy and spelling h/wk.

ME: All things, diary etc. (ref. JOBS) for next visit.

Text 6

Teaching practice observation day

June 18th, 2004

I was sent to Nelson Street Primary School for my first observation day. I arrived at 8.30 a.m. to be met by the Head Teacher, Mrs Castle. After that, I was taken to meet my mentor, Mr Baverstock, Class Teacher of Year 5.

Before the children arrived, I was set my tasks, to be completed before the next observation day:

- observe closely all teaching;
- assist the children, sitting with them during group working sessions;
- make a named seating plan of the classroom;
- select two children for close study work; and
- write a diary of the day.

The register was called at 8.55 a.m. After that, any necessary dinner money, notes and forms were collected. As soon as possible, the children's line, which was formed in the classroom, was led to the hall by Mr Baverstock.

During the walk to the hall, silence was maintained. This continued when the children sat on the floor in rows behind Year 4, to wait for Mrs Castle. Teachers did not leave until Mrs Castle had arrived.

During Assembly, the lessons, classrooms and resources had to be made ready for the first lesson. I noticed that when the children returned at 9.30 a.m., an immediate start to the Literacy lesson was thereby made possible.

The literacy lesson involved initial teaching and text study, followed by independent punctuation work. Adult help was shared among the groups. Break began at 10.45 a.m. and lasted fifteen minutes; playground duty is assigned to Mr Baverstock and me every Thursday.

The second half of the morning was taken up by Numeracy. The unit of work – to last four weeks – was symmetry. '*Gorn on Maths*' textbooks were used, so the children were given the opportunity to work at an individual pace until lunch at 12.15 p.m. However, the teachers' lunchtime did not begin until resources had been prepared for the afternoon.

The afternoon was not broken up. After registration at 1.15 p.m., and silent reading by children and adults until 1.30 p.m., two separate subjects were taught. In History, interesting group discussions on Victorian schools were prompted by a stimulating television serial. Then the last hour of the day was taken up by ICT. I was impressed by the children's confidence when using a newspaper program. Finally, the children were reminded about homework tasks, before being dismissed once the final bell was rung at 3.30 p.m.

My main conclusion drawn from the day was the need for preparation. This was particularly obvious when resources such as televisions, overhead projectors or computers were being used. In the end, I was overawed by how much work was needed by the Class Teacher, in order that every session was given a calm, peaceful start.

Text 7

The Diary of Dora Roberts – Thursday

Thursday, February 23rd, 1888

What a day I have had! First, the children were uncommonly quarrelsome and my duties seemed more than usually difficult. Secondly, the older girls would not share the doll's house; Master James grew tired of his writing; and Baby Louise cried for most of the day. As a result, I was forced to wheel her perambulator for many hours in the grounds, in spite of the freezing conditions, with the other children unwillingly accompanying me. Although I had wrapped them up well in coats, hats and boots, they complained bitterly of the cold. However, I dared not return to the house with the baby making such a noise, for the Mistress is soon to have another child, and I know she needs her rest.

At last the baby fell asleep and we returned to the nursery. However, it then required great haste to attend to all the necessary tasks. Fortunately, and because of willing assistance from Molly, the new under-nursemaid, the children were fed and changed ready to be taken down to see their parents at the appointed time. When I collected the children an hour later and took them back up to their rooms to prepare for the night, I was more than usually exhausted.

Molly's arrival has made such a difference to my life here. She is younger than I – only just 14 – and so very cheerful. Whenever the young serving boys tease her, she laughs at their jokes and answers them back. However, I do notice the Housekeeper frowning at her jolly ways.

Even my tiny room is easier to bear since Molly's arrival, although it is a tight squeeze with her iron bed next to mine. We have the room next to the nursery, which is so cold and draughty that I fear it may worsen my cough. Perhaps I could summon the courage to ask the Housekeeper for another blanket, but I fear that she will think me impertinent. Molly laughs at my timid ways and says that she just says whatever comes into her head. I do so hope that she will bring no trouble upon herself... or upon me.

Text 8

The Diary of Dora Roberts – Friday

Friday, February 24rd, 1888

Little Louise woke me twice in the night. Indeed, when it was time to get up, I felt that I had had precious little rest. I fear that the baby's teeth are giving her a great deal of trouble, and there are many more still to come.

This morning the temperature had fallen even lower than yesterday's. There was ice on the inside of my window and also on the top of my pitcher. Only after I had broken through the ice was I able to wash.

The older children attended morning prayers, but Master Alfred was reprimanded severely by his father when he failed to keep still. I fear that the Mistress will blame me for the trouble her son is in. I think that she favours him above the five girls, so she will miss him sorely when he goes to school next year.

What a to-do this evening! When Molly reappeared in the nursery, she was in a most dreadful state, weeping profusely. It seems that the Butler had overheard her joking with John, one of the footmen.

"Get to your duties, Thompson," he said.

"I am just going," Molly replied.

I would never have dared to answer back in such a way, but she is so used to joking with the young men servants, that I think she perhaps forgot herself when she answered the Butler. His position is so high, I never dare to even look at him.

After that, there was a huge fuss. The Butler called dear Molly "a common cottage girl", and shouted for the Housekeeper.

"I thought these girls were selected carefully," he stormed. "This impertinent wretch of a girl is not fit to work here."

After that, Molly was sent to scrub the nursery floor, but she knows that the Housekeeper will have more to say. We both went to bed worrying about what will happen tomorrow.

Text 9

The Diary of a Dora Roberts – Saturday

Saturday, February 25rd, 1888

I awoke with the most dreadful feeling of foreboding. Poor Molly looked as if she had hardly slept and we broke through the ice in silence. As we set about our chores, the dreaded summons came, delivered by the new under-housemaid: Molly was to present herself in the back hall, where the Housekeeper was waiting to see her. Although she endeavoured to put on a brave face, the Molly who left the nursery looked a very different person from my former jolly friend.

When Molly got down to the back hall, both the Housekeeper and the Butler were awaiting her. The Housekeeper repeated the Butler's complaints; berated Molly for letting her down; and gave her final pronouncement:

"The sooner you return to your parents, the better," said the stoney-faced Housekeeper.

It was a truly heart-breaking scene. Molly returned to the nursery in a wretched state of distress. All she could do was to pack her few belongings, and leave in disgrace. She knew the reaction that awaited her: her parents are poor, country people, with a large family of younger children; they will not want an extra mouth to feed. Poor, poor Molly!

I must be so careful in my own demeanour. The Housekeeper will be watching us all even more vigilantly now. Losing my good friend has unsettled me, so I count my good fortune in having tomorrow's visit home to lift my spirits.

It has been a hard, cold month since I saw my family last. It will be a slow walk through the snow tomorrow, so I pray that little Louise will be peaceful, in order that I can be ready to leave as soon as the Master and Mistress return from morning church. The journey will be cold and arduous, but I know that it will be worth it.

I shall go to sleep now with the smell of Mother's rabbit stew in my nose, and the taste of her parkin cake in my mouth…

Text 10

Observation days

Observation days

WHEN?

1. June 18
2. June 25

WHY?

- See real teaching
- Meet classes
- Get to know children
- Choose – special study
- Some practical exp.
- Prepare for Teaching Prac.

WHERE?

- Schools list on dept. board
- All local
- Maps from Hazel

TRANSPORT

1. Independent **OR**
2. University bus

- See me if problems

POINTS TO REMEMBER

- Guest in school
- Staff names – important
- Fit in
- School rules/code
- Punctuality
- Energy – you need sleep: adapt social life!
- **DRESS**
  - Smart
  - **NO** trainers/jeans/skimpy tops

  ***N.B. No school = no teaching practice = FAILED!**

WRITTEN WORK

- Recount of day ⟶ here
- Tasks from class teachers ⟶ schools
- Stay up to date

FINAL POINTS

- University reps
- **Good luck!**

Text 11

How to make a UK route-finder

What you need

- Map of the United Kingdom
- Coloured pencils or fine felt-tipped pens
- A photocopied outline map of the UK
- Pencil
- Up-to-date road atlas
- Ruler

What to do

1 First locate these major cities:

a. Carlisle
b. Manchester
c. Leeds
d. Hull
e. Birmingham
f. London
g. Folkestone
h. Southampton
i. Bristol
j. Cardiff

2 Then mark their exact locations on your map, using different coloured circles.

3 Write the first two letters of the place names in the circles.

4 Rule pencil lines between the circles in the following order:

- Join a to b.
- Join b to c.
- Join c to d.
- Link b and e.
- Link e and f.
- Connect f to g.
- Connect f to h.
- Connect f to i.
- Join e to i.
- Join i to j.

5 Now consult the road atlas.

6 Match your straight lines with motorways marked in the atlas.

7 Write the correct motorway number beside each line on your map.

How to make the best use of your route-finder

- Make personal additions to the map:
  – mark a city close to you;
  – mark cities close to places you visit regularly;
  – add other important motorways;
  – work out which routes you will find useful;
  – list them.

Helpful tips

- Stick your map onto thin card.
- Laminate it.
- Keep it in a convenient place in the car.
- Remember to look at it!

Text 12

Check your personal fitness level

What you will need

Pen and paper
A watch/clock with a second hand or a timer
A variety of fitness equipment – such as:

- skipping rope
- step or low bench
- trampoline
- climbing frame

What to do

1. First sit down and relax.
2. Have your watch where you can see it clearly.
3. Then work out your "at-rest" heartbeat.

How?

i. First choose one of these places:
- *the inside of your wrist*
- *the side of your neck*

ii. Now place two fingers there.
iii. Wait until you can feel your pulse.
iv. Look at your watch.
v. Count how many beats of your heart (your pulse) you can feel in 1 minute.
vi. Write down that number. That is your at-rest heartbeat, your normal pulse.

4. List the exercises you are going to do.
5. Begin with a light exercise – such as, walking.
6. Do this for 1–2 minutes.
7. Stop and check your pulse again.
8. Write down the number of times your heart beats in 1 minute.

If your pulse is the same:
Proceed immediately to instruction 10.

If your pulse is now different:
Follow instruction 9.

Text 13

Check your personal fitness level (continued)

9. Wait a minute, and check your pulse again.
   - Do this until your pulse returns to its normal rate.
   - Write down how long you have had to wait.
   - Now proceed to instruction 10
10. Move on to the next exercise on your list.
11. Do it for the same length of time as the first exercise.
12. Follow instructions 7, 8 (and 9 if necessary).
13. Continue to work through your complete list of exercises.

REMEMBER

- Do every activity for the same length of time.
- Record accurately.

What to do afterwards

a) Study your results.
b) Notice when and where your pulse was slow to return to normal.
c) Find out what this means.
d) Enter the data onto a record sheet.
e) During the following week, work on your fitness, by taking more exercise.
f) Repeat the whole investigation.
g) Compare the results. Is your heart rate returning to normal more quickly?

DON'T GIVE UP!

EXERCISE MORE – AND YOU WILL GET FITTER.

Text 14

To save a file

To save a file

1. On the **File** menu of the program you are working in, click **Save**.
2. If you haven't saved your file before, type a name for the file in **File name**.

Note

- To save a copy of a file under a different name or in a different location, on the **File** menu, click **Save As**. Click the **Save in** arrow to find the drive or folder where you want to save the file, and then type the new name in the **File name** box.

To save a file with a different name or format

1. On the **File** menu of the program you are working in, click **Save As**.
2. Specify a new name or a different format for the file you are saving.

Note

- If the file was previously saved with a different name or format, that version will remain unchanged.

To copy a file or folder to a floppy disk

1. Insert the floppy disk into the disk drive.
2. Open My Documents.
   If the file or folder you want to copy is not located in My Documents or its subfolders, use Search to find it. To open Search, click **Start**, and then click **Search**.
3. Click the file or folder you want to copy.
4. Under **File and Folder Tasks**, click **Copy this file** or **Copy this folder**.
5. In **Copy Items**, click **3½ Floppy (A:)**, and then click **Copy**.

Notes

- To open My Documents, click **Start**, and then click **My Documents**.
- You can also copy a file or folder to a floppy disk by right-clicking the file or folder, pointing to **Send To**, and then clicking **3½ Floppy (A)**.

Microsoft Corporation

Text 15

How does the human respiratory system function?

The respiratory system is made up of your lungs and the passages that lead to them. When you breathe air into your lungs, oxygen from the air passes into your blood, which carries it around your body. The oxygen mixes with digested food to give you energy. Carbon dioxide is breathed out as waste.

HOW RESPIRATION WORKS

When you breathe in, air is sucked through your nose or mouth and down your windpipe. The lining of your nose and windpipe make a slippery liquid called mucus. This warms and moistens the air, so it can travel more easily along the passages. It also traps dirt and germs in the air. Tiny hairs called cilia waft the mucus away from your lungs towards your nose and throat.

Your windpipe divides into two tubes (called bronchi), and one leads to each lung. Your lungs are made up of a network of tubes, called bronchioles. They get narrower as they branch off. At the end of these tubes are clusters of millions of tiny air sacs surrounded by many blood vessels. Oxygen is passed through the thin walls of the sacs into the blood vessels, where it is absorbed into your blood.

The oxygen is carried to different parts of your body, where it is combined with nutrients that have been absorbed during digestion. This produces energy and carbon dioxide. The carbon dioxide is carried back to the lungs in your blood and you breathe it out.

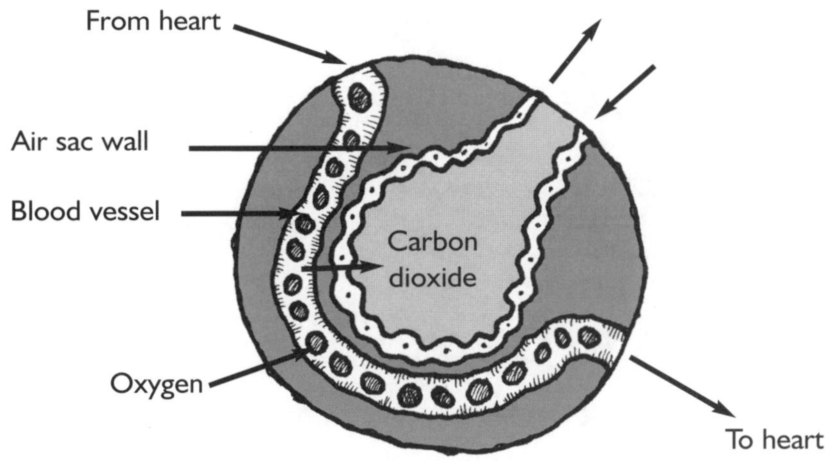

The Usborne Internet-linked Book of Knowledge

Text 16

How do people breathe?

Breathing, or ventilation, is the movement of air in and out of the lungs. It is controlled by a group of muscles in your chest, called the intercostal muscles, and a flat sheet of muscle called the diaphragm, which lies under your lungs.

As you breathe in, your intercostal muscles pull your ribs up and out, and your diaphragm flattens. This leaves space for your lungs to expand and air rushes into them.

As you breathe out, your diaphragm relaxes, so it becomes arched again. Your intercostal muscles also relax, moving your ribs down and in. The space inside your chest gets smaller again, and air is squeezed out. This is called exhalation.

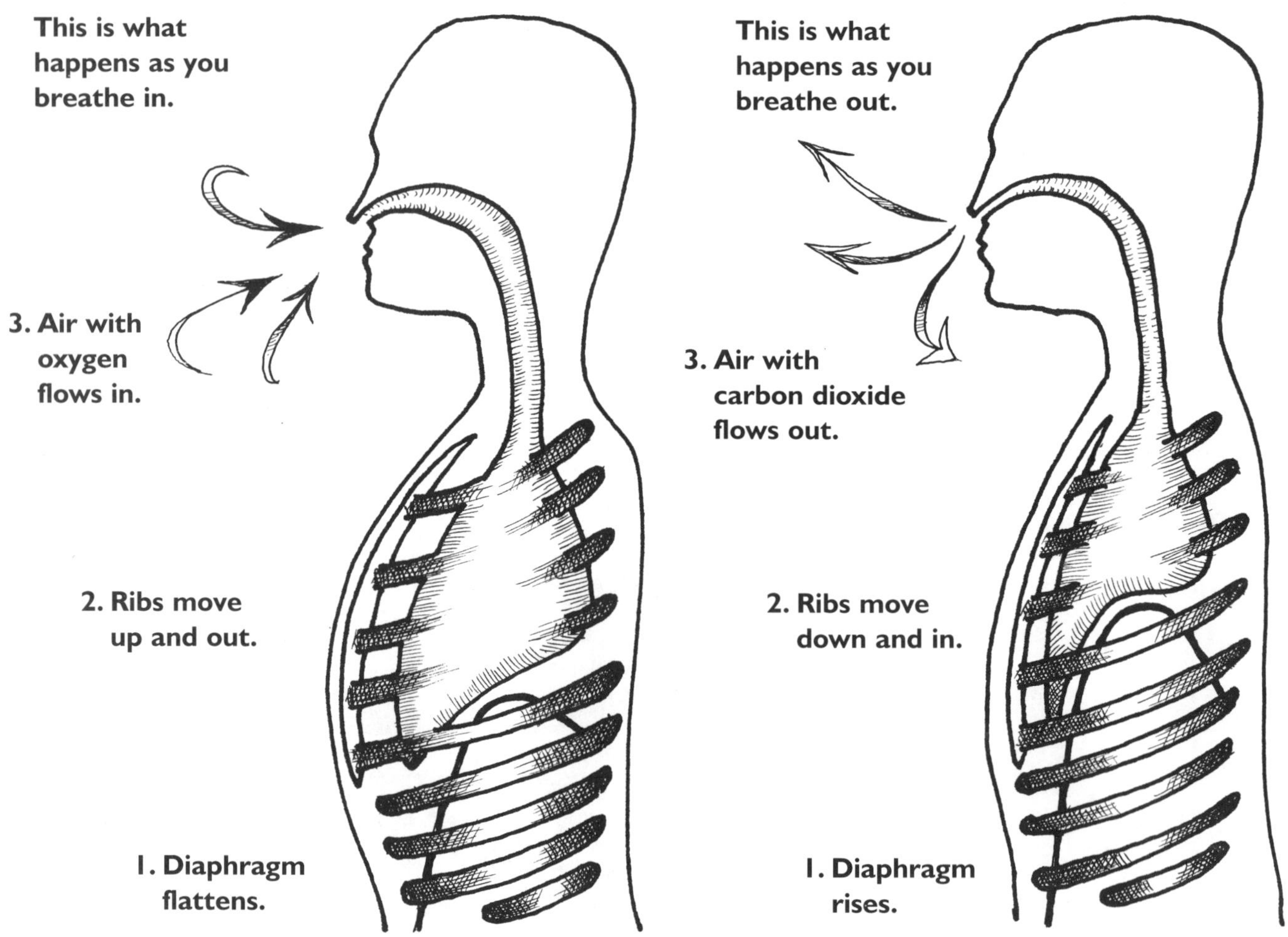

The Usborne Internet-linked Book of Knowledge

Text 17

How is sound made?

A sound is made when something vibrates, making the air around it vibrate too. The sound you hear is carried by the vibrating air as a sound wave.

SOUND WAVES

Inside a loudspeaker, a paper cone vibrates, sending sound energy into the air. As the cone moves forwards, it presses together air particles in front of it. As it moves back, it leaves an area where the particles are more spaced out.

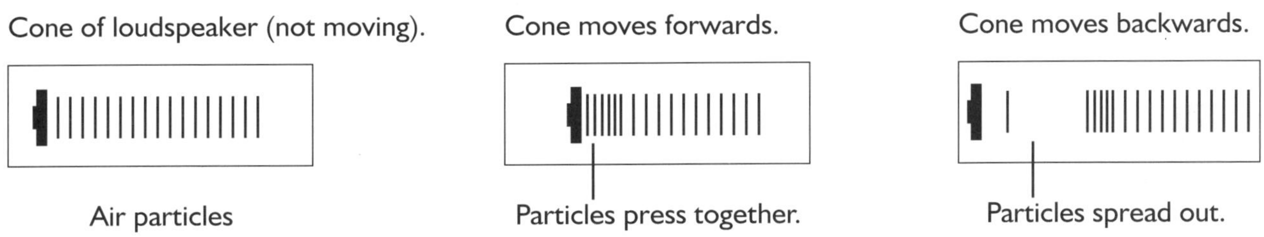

Sound waves can be shown as a wavy line of ups and downs, or peaks and troughs. The peaks show where particles have been squashed. The troughs show where particles are spread out.

PITCH AND FREQUENCY

The faster something vibrates, the higher the sound it makes. The slower it vibrates, the lower the sound. The number of vibrations something makes per second is called the frequency, or pitch, of the sound. Frequency is measured in hertz (Hz).

Bees beat their wings 200 times a second, so the sound you hear has a frequency of 200Hz. Mosquitoes make a higher-pitched sound than bees because they beat their wings faster, about 500 times per second. Humans can only hear sounds that are between 20Hz and 20,000Hz.

LOUDNESS

A loud sound makes big vibrations. The size of a vibration is called its amplitude so the louder the sound, the bigger the amplitude.

Loudness is measured in units called decibels (dB), named after A. G. Bell, the inventor of the telephone. The blue whale is the loudest animal in the world. It makes sounds of up to 188dB, which can be picked up over 850km (530 miles) away.

The Usborne Internet-linked Book of Knowledge

Text 18

Notes on sound changes

<u>Ref. Bk: The Usborne Internet-linked Book Of Knowledge</u>

Changes in vibrations → Sound changes
Vibrations faster = higher sound
Vibr. slower = lower s.

<u>PITCH</u> = difference between high/low sounds

Pitch - also called **FREQUENCY**
Frequency/pitch = how many vibr. per sec.
F. measured in Hz (hertz)

<u>EXAMPLE:</u>
Bees beat wings 200 times per sec.
↓
sound has f. of 200Hz

V. high noise: mosquito (wings go 500 a sec!)
People can hear 20–20 000Hz. Not higher/lower

<u>LOUDNESS</u>
Loud sound = <u>big</u> vibrations
AMPLITUDE means vibration size
Loudness measured in DECIBELS (dB) – after <u>Bell</u>, phone inventor
<u>NB:</u> Blue whale = loudest animal: 188dB sound – noise travels 850km
Loudness can hurt human ears

Text 19

How are sounds changed?

Sound changes are caused by changes in vibrations. If vibrations become faster, then the sound made becomes higher. When vibrations get slower, so the sound produced is lowered.

PITCH AND FREQUENCY

The variation in the range of a sound is called its pitch. Pitch, or frequency, is determined by vibration speed. This speed, which is calculated per second, is measured in hertz, normally abbreviated as Hz.

For example, if a bee's wings are moved at a speed of 200 times a second, then the sound heard is said to have a frequency of 200Hz. In the same way, the sound produced by a mosquito, which beats its wings 500 times a second, is measured at 500Hz. Consequently, it is heard by the human ear as a high-pitched whine.

The human ear is not designed to cope with sounds outside a particular range: in order for a sound to be audible to human beings, it must be between 20Hz and 20 000Hz.

VOLUME

Volume is the loudness of a sound. This is dependent on the size of the vibrations. If a sound is loud, it means that the vibrations are big. The size of vibrations is referred to as the "amplitude" of a sound. Therefore, the louder a sound is, so the bigger is its amplitude.

Alexander Bell, who invented the telephone, is remembered in the unit of measurement. Consequently, loudness is measured in decibels (dB). The loudest of animal sounds, which is produced by the blue whale, is measured at 188dB. The amplitude results in a sound that can be heard a staggering 850km away.

Adapted from *The Usborne Internet-linked Book of Knowledge*

Text 20

How do rivers shape the land?

The landscape can be changed by rivers. The three processes responsible are:

- erosion;
- transportation;
- deposition.

Erosion
Erosion refers to the wearing away of land. In upland areas, the river can gradually wear away land and create valleys.

Transportation
Transportation refers to the movement of material by the river. The river has the strength to carry rocks, boulders and trees.

Deposition
Deposition is the shedding of material by the river. When the river drops deposits of mud and sand, these deposits form banks or small islands.

As a river flows downhill, it carries with it stones, sand, pebbles and tiny fragments of rock which it has collected in the hills and mountains of its source. As the loose material is carried along by the river, so the stones and pieces of rock cut into and scrape against the bed and banks of the river: the result is that the bed deepens and widens as it becomes worn away.

When rainfall is heavy, the river level rises and its water flows more quickly. Power increases, giving the river the strength to uproot trees or dislodge boulders.

As the river travels downstream, its water carries more and more mud. If too much deposit builds up, the water can no longer sustain its load. As the river slows down, at the point at which it enters the sea, it drops the deposits of sediment, sometimes resulting in the formation of a **delta**.

Nevertheless, such landscape changes are not readily noticeable. The river's effect on the landscape is very gradual, and visible changes to the landscape are likely to take thousands or even millions of years. Over such an extended period of geological time, whole hills may be worn away and coastlines altered. However, abrupt change does sometimes occur.

In August 1952, 220 mm of rain fell in Devon in 24 hours; freak storms hit the county. Rivers burst their banks and swept down hillsides. Without warning and at terrifying speed, the town of Lynmouth was devastated: its roads and bridges were swept away; houses were buried beneath a flow of rocks, mud and uprooted trees; its river cut a completely new course. In one night, permanent change was made.

Text 21

How do coasts change?

Coastlines are not fixed; they remain in a state of change. Over a period of many years, a country's coastline may alter significantly in shape, as its coast is worn down or built up by the effect of water.

Water is a source of **energy**. When a sea is at its roughest and waves are at their highest, that energy is a powerful force, capable of moving rocks and large stones. However, when the sea is calm and its waves are small, the energy is so low that no more than sand can be dislodged.

There are two distinct types of waves.

Destructive waves

Destructive waves occur when the sea is at its stormiest. They break with force against a cliff, causing pieces of it to break away. This is **erosion**.

The destructive energy of the waves is increased by pebbles and small stones the waves collected as they grew bigger. By the time the waves are hurled against the cliff, these pebbles have become a sharp weapon. When the pebbles land against the base of the cliff, they cut into it and begin the process of wearing the cliff away. This is called **abrasion**.

Constructive waves

Constructive waves are waves that occur when a wave breaks onto a flat area. The wave loses speed: in so doing, it releases the pebbles and small stones it is carrying. These pebbles and small stones are moved around and ground down, becoming smaller and finer: the result is the gradual construction of a sandy beach.

Coasts can change also because of a change in sea level. For many years, scientists have expressed concerns about **global warming**. They have warned that many of the processes of modern living result in pollution that increases the **greenhouse gases** in the atmosphere. Greenhouse gases contribute to a rise in temperature.

Scientists fear that rises in temperatures could bring changes to the world and its different climates. If the temperature rise were to occur in the polar regions, ice would melt and this would result in a rise in the sea level. Scientists have observed already that our sea level is currently rising by about 1mm per year. In the future, more land is likely to disappear below sea level, and the shape of coastlines will be changed.

Text 22

Family life in Victorian Britain

CONTENTS

INDEX

Richard Wood

Text 23

Family gatherings

Middle-class family gatherings were often rather formal occasions. A strong sense of family values was important to the Victorians, so a lot of effort was usually made for family gatherings. Traditional social customs played an important part at these gatherings.

MEALTIMES

Mealtimes gave Victorian families a chance to meet together regularly. Meals were quite formal. Father sat at the head of the table, mother at the foot, and the children sat round the sides. Meals did not start until the youngest child said **grace** to thank God for providing food for the table. In better-off homes, a servant helped to pass the dishes and fill glasses. In other families the older daughters did this job.

Middle-class families ate well. Even a 'plain' family dinner started with soup or fish – herrings were very popular. Meats such as boiled rabbits, roast duck or Irish stew followed. To finish there were puddings, fruit tarts or cheese. If guests were invited, the meal was a much grander affair. There could be six courses, each eaten with separate plates and cutlery.

CELEBRATIONS

Christenings, weddings and funerals were chances for larger family groups to get together. People normally lived quite close to their relatives, but any relations from further away could now arrive easily by train. When someone died, the whole family wore black **mourning** clothes. A widow was expected to wear black for a year, then purple 'half mourning' for a second year. She even wore black jewellery and wrote letters on black-edged paper during this period.

Christmas was a happy family occasion. Prince Albert set up a Christmas tree for the royal children at Windsor Castle. Other families copied the idea and soon this became a popular custom all over Britain. Christmas cards and crackers, plum pudding and Christmas cake, and visits from Santa Claus are other customs which were started by Victorian families.

Richard Wood

Text 24

Family outings

PERFORMANCES

Many Victorian families must have looked forward to Boxing Day, when the pantomime season began. Parents and children crowded into the gas-lit theatres to enjoy the songs, dances and silly jokes of shows like *Cinderella* or *Jack and the Beanstalk*. Sometimes there would be a fair, or a circus. The children gasped at the dangerous acts of the trapeze artists and lion tamers.

Punch and Judy shows, complete with crocodiles, policemen and sausages, were very popular for children's parties. Music-hall variety shows also became popular from the 1880s. However, most people did not think that these were at all suitable for ladies or children because of their cheeky songs and rude jokes.

By 1900 the first moving films were on show. Despite the silent, jerky pictures and piano accompaniments, these early films must have excited families all over Britain.

Punch and Judy shows were popular with Victorian children. You will find the same characters in modern-day shows.

HOLIDAYS

In 1871, three **bank holidays** were introduced to give families a short break from work. Many people had never been further than a day's walk from home. The bank holiday gave them a chance to make a day trip by train to a seaside town like Blackpool or Margate.

Longer breaks from work were unheard of for most people. But many middle-class families now spent a week or two in fashionable 'watering places' like Brighton, Bath or Cromer. Even on the beach, they wore smart, formal clothes. They swam from horse-drawn bathing-machines (like little sheds on wheels) to avoid being seen going down to the beach in their bathing costumes. Men and boys usually bathed naked, so they used a separate part of the beach well out of sight of the ladies!

Richard Wood

Text 25

Children

Speak roughly to your little child,
And beat him when he sneezes.
He only does it to annoy,
Because he knows it teases.

The Victorians were very concerned about how to bring up children. Popular magazines like *Mother's Assistant, The Home Friend* and *Family Treasure* were full of advice and practical tips.

Some said that children were naturally good and should be treated kindly to bring out the best in them. Others argued that children were born "full of wickedness" and should be beaten to make them obedient. "Spare the rod and spoil the child" (meaning that a child who was not beaten would grow up to be spoilt) was a popular family saying. Cautionary tales, like *Harriet and the Matches*, showed children what would happen if they were disobedient.

Some children were cruelly treated and in 1889 the National Society for the Prevention of Cruelty to Children (NSPCC) was founded to help them. However, in most families children were loved, though treated rather severely by today's standards. Stories like *Harriet and the Matches* were used by parents to frighten children into doing as they were told.

WORKING CHILDREN

Childhood did not last long for many poor children. They were forced by their parents to work long hours in factories, down mines, as servants or as chimney sweeps. In the country, many children worked in gangs on the land. This work was terribly hard and after 1867 it was against the law for children under the age of eight to do this kind of work.

From the 1830s onwards, many new laws were passed to try and control children's working hours and conditions. After 1870, most children attended school until they were ten years old. This was unpopular with many parents as well as children because it meant a drop in the family income. Even in 1901, the year Queen Victoria died, 300,000 children under ten were still working up to forty hours per week. But in most families, childhood was longer and more pleasant than ever before.

Richard Wood

Text 26

Index

Robert Nicholson from Great Civilisations

Text 27

Philosophers and scientists

The Ancient Greeks were very curious about themselves and the world around them and made many important advances in science, learning and art. Great thinkers were known as **philosophers** no matter what subject they studied. The word philosophy comes from the Greek words for 'love of wisdom'. Philosophers tried to find out how the universe worked, why people were good or evil, and how people should live their lives.

Many Greek discoveries provide the foundations of our knowledge and beliefs. Greeks studied the stars and discovered that the Earth floated freely in space, turning on its own axis. They also correctly predicted eclipses of the sun. Sometimes they were wrong. Ptolemy, a Greek scholar, thought the Earth was the centre of the Universe.

Most new ideas were never used for solving practical problems. Metal-working techniques, for example, were still primitive and never developed enough to make tools which could take advantage of the advances made in science.

Famous Philosophers

- **Hippocrates** (about 460–377 BC)
  Hippocrates founded a medical school, where he practised scientific medicine instead of magic or religion. He taught the value of knowing how the body worked.
- **Aristotle** (384–322 BC)
  Aristotle examined living things in nature. He also wrote on many subjects, including politics, and invented a method of thinking called logic.
- **Socrates** (about 469–399 BC)
  Socrates, one of the first great philosophers of Classical Greece, taught the value of questioning common beliefs in order to find new ideas and explore new truths.
- **Plato** (about 427–347 BC)
  Plato founded a school for philosophers called The Academy where he taught Aristotle. His famous books are The Republic *and* Dialogues.

The Greek philosopher Eratosthenes calculated the circumference of the Earth by measuring the angle of the sun at Alexandria in northern Egypt, and measuring the distance from there to Syene in southern Egypt, where the sun was overhead at noon. His figure for the circumference was correct to within 320km.

Robert Nicholson from Great Civilisations

Text 28

Arts and crafts in Ancient Greece

The Greeks thought that there was a perfect shape for any object whether it was a simple clay pot or a huge temple. They used both mathematics and ideas about what is good in art, known as **aesthetics**, to try to make their art as beautiful as possible.

The Greeks made beautiful elegant pots covered in patterns and paintings. Many were used every day, for storing water, oil, or wine, but some of the most beautiful pots were kept carefully and then buried with the dead.

Greek statues were made from stone or bronze. Early statues were not lifelike, but as the skills of the sculptors developed, they became graceful, with expressive faces and clothes which look real. Most stone statues were painted, but have now lost their colour.

The Parthenon in Athens is one of the finest Greek buildings still standing. It is made from carved blocks of cream-coloured marble, held together with wooden pegs and metal clamps. Each side is decorated with rows of columns, typical of Greek architecture. This Classical style has been copied all over the world. Is there a building like this near where you live?

Robert Nicholson from Great Civilisations

Text 29

Arts and the Ancient Greeks

The Ancient Greeks were renowned for their interest and achievements in the fields of mathematics, architecture and science.

Architecture

Their architectural style followed the principles of simplicity and symmetry. They invented the classical style. These classical buildings by the Ancient Greeks were likely to bear certain features:

- grandeur was added by the use of steps leading up to the main entrance;
- a carved, patterned border, often made up of statues, formed a frieze;
- the roof had a triangular support;
- columns, often carved to resemble women, were usually present;
- the tops of the columns were carved in one of three distinctive styles – Doric, Ionic or Corinthian.

The classical style that the Ancient Greeks developed has continued to be admired and imitated by architects.

Mathematics and science

Mathematicians today still use the teaching of the Greek mathematicians, Pythagoras and Euclid. Their theories and rules are referred to and their discoveries of basic principles underpin much of today's work in the field of geometry.

Archimedes' Principle is a basic scientific principle, essential to the understanding of weight and the displacement of liquid. Its name is a reminder that it was Archimedes, a Greek mathematician and engineer, who discovered this principle of buoyancy. Archimedes was also of immediate, practical help to his people: he invented many engines of war used by the Greeks in their battles against the Romans.

Art

The Ancient Greeks were also great artists. They excelled as potters, producing ornate vases from their local clay. The clay became a red colour once fired, and it provided the background for intricate, decorative detail. Emphasis was placed on the beauty of this decoration, with scenes from ordinary life, battles and famous tales often depicted on the pots.

The pottery produced by the ancient Greeks was not just ornamental: it was also functional. Jars were created for the storage of oil and wine. These kitchen pots were less likely to be decorated, as they were often intended for the export of olive oil and wine overseas.

Text 30

The newly-delivered leaflet sounds interesting...

JIM'S GYM

Would you like to be as fit as this?

Silly question – of course you would!
Just call in and see Jim – the local body expert

- EXCELLENT EQUIPMENT
  You name it – we've got it! All brand-new, top-of-the-range fitness aids
- FANTASTIC FACILITIES
  Sauna, sunbeds, beauty treatments, nutritional and homeopathic care
- TERRIFIC TRAINERS
  Personal attention promised from highly-qualified staff
- REASONABLE RATES:
  We're too embarrassed to print them!
  Even we think they're too low!

SPECIAL OPENING OFFER
FOR FIRST 100 APPLICANTS
LIMITED PLACES LEFT

Call in NOW for the facts!

Jim's Gym
5 Spender Street (Off Crock Place), Lilworth

SPRING CLEANERS

The professional team

Woodwork polished **Not a speck of dust missed**

Every surface left gleaming

Let's face it – you're busy.
What have you got?
- **a demanding job**
- **friends and family**
- **a fun social life**

Don't you deserve a break?
We can give it to you:
- **equipment supplied**
- **hours to suit you**
- **full insurance cover**
- **economical rates**

And you still want to stay in cleaning?
Get out and enjoy yourself!

Forget housework – let *SPRING CLEANERS* do it – that's our job!

Let US take the strain – YOU won't regret it
Ring Kylie or Krystle today

08100 374259

Text 32

Cruelty in the countryside

Over 1000 fox hunts organised last year!

5000 terrified foxes killed!

Farmland trampled on and ruined

Crops destroyed in chase

1. Hunting is a minority sport, with no benefits.
2. Scientific tests prove that the animals feel terror.
3. Animals' rights are being violated. The Government needs to act **NOW**.

1+2+3 = BAN IT!

Join ***CARING CAMPAIGN***
on **Saturday May 5th** for a public protest.
BE THERE!

Coaches leave for London from all main coach stations at 7.00 a.m. – back at 9.00 p.m.

CARING CAMPAIGN **– voice of the Moral Majority**

The Country Dweller

Of course you enjoy the beauty of Workshire!

You must do – you chose to make your life here. So why don't you want to stay? You may not know it, but an enemy is getting ready to drive you away:

THE FOX

- 5 years ago: the fox population of this county was under control.
- 2 years ago: a 15% increase was beginning to cause concern.
- Today: a further 15% increase in numbers takes us to the brink of a county crisis.

Do any of us want to reach that crisis point?

So – what can we do?

In fact, the answer is not that difficult, but it does require common sense. Surely we all have that!
The answer lies in **CONTROL**.

Licensed hunting, controlled by government permits, is the way forward. That way a manageable fox population allows all other country dwellers to keep themselves and their homes safe.

Without the means of control we could face:

- a threat to our rural livelihood;
- unprotected small livestock;
- diminished farmers' rights;
- our lives changed.

Think about it: you will realise it makes sense.

Hunting must stay
Find ***The Country Dweller*** caravan on Saturday, in Digbeth Market Square, and sign the petition.

VOTE Orange

the easy vote

Who are we?

Jane Bourne

Rob Flixton

Karen Haggit

How do we know what you want?

We are all local people, so we all understand local problems. For too long, city commuters have been speaking for you.

Recognise it: you need a change.

Think about these facts:

- Our children attend the same schools – including the ones that need more facilities.
- We all use the same local shops, so we know about the shortage of car parks.
- We suffer the same terrible traffic and transport problems.
- We know what it is really like to live here.
- **Naturally, we should be the people to represent you**.

What do we stand for?

✔ We believe in fairness, which means an equal chance for all of us.
✔ We want free nursery places, so that parents can choose when and where to work.
✔ We expect home carers for our elderly relatives.
✔ We will petition for improved playing areas for our children.
✔ We will badger the Government to provide proper public transport.
✔ **We will get you a decent standard of life.**

When can you choose us?

Council Elections are on **May 16th**. You have 3 votes: make them count.

VOTE ORANGE

the easy vote

Text 35

Classworks

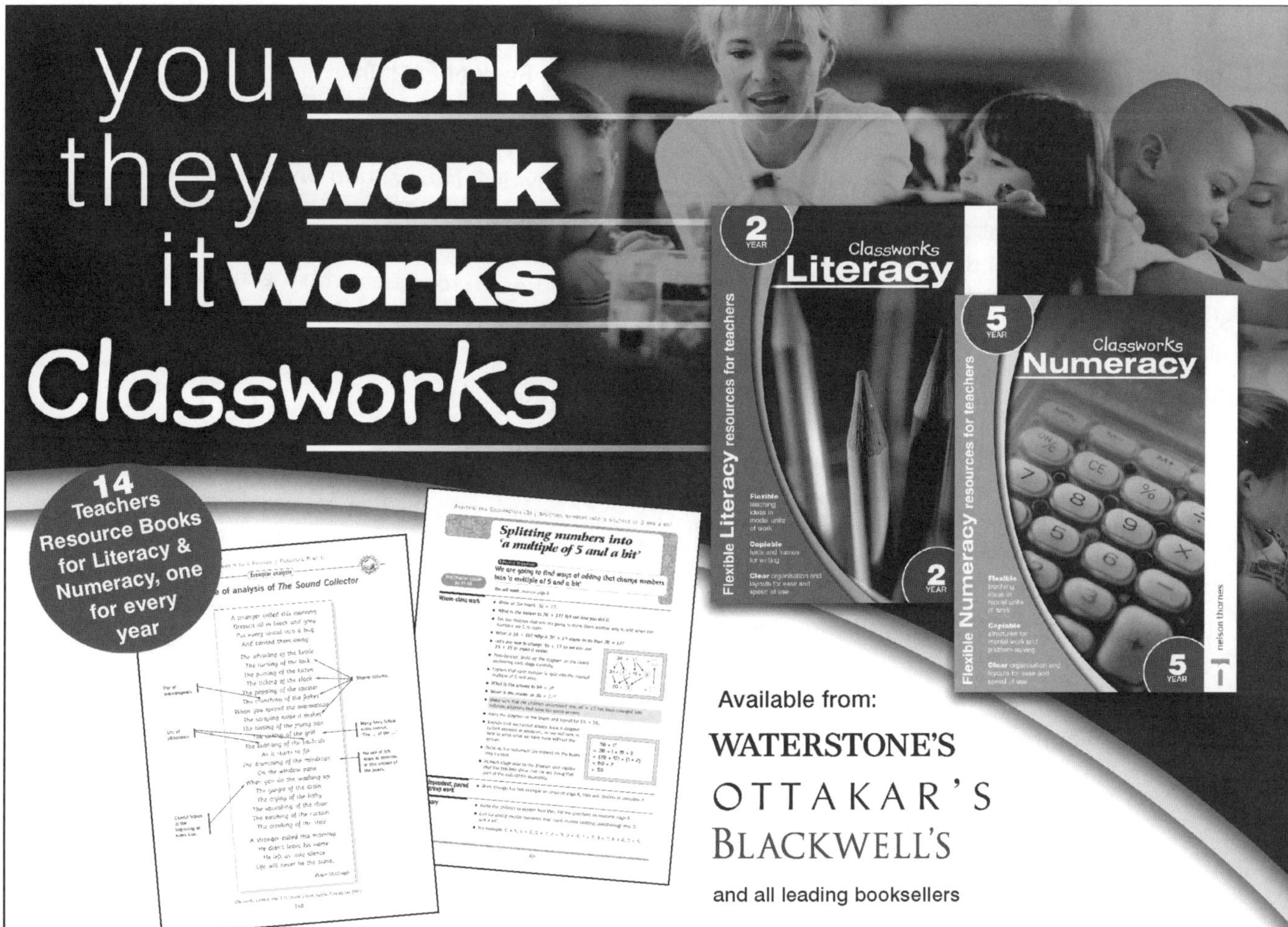

Classworks is a brand new teacher's resource series designed for the way you teach Primary Literacy and Numeracy now. It gives you flexible ideas, not prescriptive lessons. In blocked units, to fit with the latest thinking on curriculum delivery.

Each book covers either Literacy or Numeracy. There's a book for the year you teach.

And that's about it.

No filling, no padding, no waffle. Just all the nuts and bolts you need for great lessons, built the way you want them.

- Bulleted text
- Clear headings and outcomes
- Loads of structured photocopiables
- Everything on one page

Classworks teacher's resource books.
For effective lessons, built by you.

nelson thornes

Order Today! Simply complete the coupon below and send it to:
Primary Customer Services, Nelson Thornes, FREEPOST SWC 0507 Cheltenham GL53 7ZZ
or call customer services on 01242 267280 Fax 01242 253695

Text 36

Educational Visits

Edinburgh Butterfly and Insect World

Whatever the weather, summer or winter, stroll through the wonderful world of an exotic rainforest, a landscape of tropical plants surrounding splashing waterfalls and pools. Enjoy the great pleasure of watching hundreds of the world's most spectacular and colourful butterflies flying all around you.

Share the world of the butterfly as they fly, sip nectar, court, egg lay or simply bask in the sunlight showing off their glorious colours. You can also marvel at the industrious leaf-cutting ants, handle weird and wonderful minibeasts (if you dare!). Not to be handled, but fascinating to view, are a selection of deadly scorpions.

The Bank of England

The Bank of England offers a comprehensive educational service providing information on its current and historic role. The service includes organised group visits to the Bank's Museum, together with a general enquiry service to assist students and teachers with their studies/research.

Presentations

Various presentations, which take place in the Museum cinema, are available to groups of between 15 and 45 in number. All of the presentations are free of charge, but must be booked in advance. All presentations last approximately one hour, although additional time should be allowed to visit the Museum.

Brief details about each of the presentations are listed below:

- **Film/Question and Answer session** – suitable for groups with a current interest in the Bank – in particular, students of economics, business studies, banking and finance.
- **Money presentation** – catering for younger visitors. Two variations of this presentation are available, suitable for 5-10 year olds and 11-14 year olds, respectively. Plenty of audience participation!
- **Audio visual presentation** – suitable for groups with a general interest in the Bank. The presentation covers the following areas:
- the Bank's history and architecture
- banknotes
- gold
- the Bank today

Lochwinnoch Nature Reserve

Situated within the Clyde-Muirshiel Regional Park, Lochwinnoch is one of the few remaining wetland sites in west Scotland. The visitor centre, with its viewing tower and telescopes, gives good views over the marshland and loch, where in the winter you may see a wide variety of wildfowl and goosanders. In the spring, great crested grebes and lapwings can be seen displaying and sedge warblers can be heard singing in the marshland. The reserve is ideal for all the family, as the trails, birdwatching hides and visitor centre are easily accessible. A programme of events is run throughout the year. You can also enjoy a light snack or browse in the RSPB shop.

Opening Times

Reserve open at all times; visitor centre open daily 10 a.m. to 5 p.m. (closed 25 and 26 December and 1 and 2 January).

Text 37

Educational Visits (continued)

Warwick Castle

Warwick Castle has almost 1000 years of history, brought vividly to life… so where better to excite the imagination of your pupils, whilst satisfying the requirements of the National Curriculum?

Opening Times

The Castle is open every day (except Christmas Day), 10 a.m. – 6 p.m. April to September, 10 a.m. – 5 p.m. October to March. Last admission half an hour before closing.

Elsecar Heritage Centre

The Living History Centre

The Living History Centre has been specially designed to bring history to life exploring society, fashions, schooling, industry, and every day household items from the early 1800s to the 1960s. Children can smell the past, take part in a Victorian melodrama on the specially built theatre and find out how to do your washing in the 1850s and 1940s.

The Living History Centre provides resources to cover various elements within the History programme of study for Key Stages 1–4, including chronology of social and industrial history, Victorian Britain, Britain since 1930, Britain from 1750–c1900, and the twentieth century world. The session includes worksheets for Key Stages 1–4.

Length of sessions: 1–1½ hours.

The Centre is suitable for a maximum of 35 pupils (additional numbers on discussion).

Cost – £1.20 each.

One adult free for every 10 children booked. Additional adults £1.20. All accompanying helpers are free for groups with special needs.

Elsecar Heritage Centre

The Victorian Classroom

Set at the turn of the century, the session explores what life was like in the Victorian age. Children are "taught" by a member of the Elsecar Team and led through the interactive "lessons". The session looks at home and school life, everyday objects, and the changes in conditions and objects compared with the modern day.

Queen Victoria's life and achievements are explored, as well as those of inventors and engineers of the era, which includes looking at the growth of the railways, coal mining, ironworks, and the local Earls Fitzwilliam. Session for KS1–2.

Victorian classroom is suitable for a maximum of 34 pupils (minimum 15 children).

Cost – £2.20.

One adult free for every 10 children booked. Additional adults £2.20.

Text 38

Dear Mr Jewell

27 Walnut Road,
Chestnut Estate,
Lilworth,
Woodshire,
CV2 1AT

4th April 2004

Dear Mr Jewell,

I just want to say what a smashing place your gym is. Already my doctor has seen an improvement in my health, and that is after only ten visits. Clearly, your fitness centre is going to be worth any number of medicines.

Lilworth had no gym before yours opened, so you have done us a great service. I like the fact there are plenty of different machines, meaning that when one is not working, I can easily use another one. After all, it stands to reason that, if equipment is getting frequent use, there are bound to be some breakdowns.

Unfortunately, some people always expect perfection, but that just shows they are not thinking logically and are not willing to be reasonable. The truth about those people is that they will moan about anything, however hard anyone tries to please them.

I am impressed, as well, by your willingness to listen to the members' suggestions: my girlfriend spoke to you about the beauty salon and, two days later, it had been repainted. I do not think anyone could ask for better service than that.

Thanks again for this great facility – keep up the good work.

Yours sincerely,

Chris Dyer

Text 39

Dear Sir

Commodore Bungalow
Elite Drive
Lilworth
Woodshire

April 5th 2004

The Manager
Jim's Gym
Spender Street
Lilworth
Woodshire

Dear Sir

I am clearly the victim of an April fool joke! I cannot, for one moment, believe that the building described in your leaflet, and Spender Street's gymnasium, which I am now unfortunate enough to be a member of, are one and the same place.

How dare you, Sir, commit such fraud against the public! Does the establishment I visited today have "fantastic facilities" or "excellent equipment"? No. In reality, a dirty, disgusting bacteria-filled slum holds the poorest and cheapest of fitness-attaining items! Lies, have been told, in order that profit can be made.

As for the training staff, are we members realistically meant to believe that they are highly-qualified? No sane individual could possibly believe those badly-spoken, ill-kempt youths, barely of working age, could have passed any rigorous examination.

In consequence of the deceit that has now come to light, I am chairing a meeting of members tomorrow evening, with a view to regaining our subscriptions. If money is not returned promptly, legal action will, as a result, be taken. Your robbery, Sir, will not go unpunished!

Reginald Fawcett-Major, OBE

Text 40

Dear Mrs Perkins... (1)

Mrs Perkins is trying to choose a place to visit with her Year 5 class. In desperation, she has said that she will agree with the person who writes the most persuasive letter.

15th May 2004

Dear Mrs Perkins,

My vote is for The Bank of England. After all, everyone in this class is interested in money. No sensible person wants to end up in a financial mess: therefore, it is vital to learn how to manage money.

As well as that, it is essential to know how the country's money is handled, where it is kept and if it is really safe. The visit will teach us about England's finances; this is important knowledge for every child. How else can they grow up to be responsible citizens?

Naturally, 10-year-olds cannot be expected to understand very difficult financial problems, but a visit to The Bank of England would be an excellent way to start learning. If children of our age can get to find out more about how the country's budget is run, then there is probably a good chance of the next generation of adults making a better job of running the country's economy.

As well as education about money, there would also be the opportunity to see London – a first visit for many people in this class. It would not be difficult to combine a visit to The Bank with a visit to other places of interest in London. As a result, the trip would have even greater educational value.

I hope you will agree with my choice.

Yours sincerely,

Emily Girhan

Text 41

Dear Mrs Perkins... (2)

15th May 2004

Dear Mrs Perkins,

I believe that *At-Bristol* is the obvious choice for us. My parents do not believe in wasting school time, so I would not be allowed to go on a school trip unless the place had a first-class reputation, as I know is the case here. This centre's activities, whilst being excellent science work, sound stimulating and exciting, which will satisfy my parents, as they can be sure there will be no boredom.

Have you thought about two of the most important considerations: time and cost? Our school is only 15 miles away from Bristol, which means that the coach journey to *At-Bristol,* which is the closest of all these places, would be a sensible length. As a result, the school would only need to hire a coach for a short period at the beginning and end of the day, leaving more real learning time. Do we really want to waste a school day, sitting on a coach for any longer than necessary?

Because the coach would be hired for only a short period, the charge, which would be made by the coach company to the school, should be small. Then, how much can you reasonably ask us to contribute? I know that many of my friends could not afford an expensive trip, so cost is an essential consideration.

Finally, too many places, as I have seen from trips during other years, are not properly set up for Key Stage 2 education. In the case of *At-Bristol*, it is stated clearly in the leaflet that there are "endless educational opportunities"; this is a very strong point in favour of this centre. After all, what would be the point in going on an educational visit that did not turn out to be educational?

You can see that *At-Bristol* is our only safe choice. With so much in its favour, what would be the point of considering anywhere else?

Yours sincerely,

Melanie Stokes

Text 42

Dear Mrs Perkins... (3)

14 Market Street,
Grove Estate,
Oakham,
CR5 1FH.

June 3rd, 2004

Dear Mrs Perkins,

May I have a few moments of your attention? Unfortunately, that attention is coming too late, but perhaps I can save other children wasting revision and examination preparation time, in the way that has occurred with your class this year.

What on earth possessed you to choose such a poor place for Year 5 science work? Education appears to have been the last thing on your mind. I accept that a day trip to Scotland is certainly an unusual idea, but nine hours in a coach offers no educational value.

Our local area abounds in well-run, child-orientated museums, science centres, and nature parks. Why should a teacher need to travel to Edinburgh for the day? If Edinburgh offers the one, particular stick insect you want to show the children, then perhaps *Edinburgh Butterfly and Insect World* could send you a photograph or video next time. It would save lesson time, and be far cheaper.

The truth is, Mrs Perkins, that you were neglecting to do your own teaching properly. All year, your planning has been poor, and this outing was just further proof of your lack of expertise. No well-organised teacher would have dreamt of squandering the children's time in that way. As it is, we parents have wasted money, and our children have lost valuable preparation time, jeopardising their chances of success in the forthcoming examination. Are you proud of yourself?

Yours sincerely

Serena M. Kalan

Serena Kalan

Text 43

An open letter

TO: All Teachers

I think you need to learn a few things about being a parent today:

1. It is **expensive**.
2. **We** take our children to plenty of places at the weekend.
3. We do not want more, **unnecessary trips** in school time.
4. We are **not** able to afford them.

When do you teachers think about us? Surely it is obvious that we already face constant demands on our money, without you adding to the burden.

Why don't you give us a break? Surely you know why we send our children to school? We expect them to learn, not to play. So where do we want them to learn? We want our children to learn **in** school, of course.

The National Curriculum is there for **YOU** to teach – not an untrained curator at a museum. You are the professional paid to educate, so you should be the one doing the job. Surely you cannot expect to be paid for a day out?

I hope that other parents will join me in taking a strong stand against these time-wasting outings. Naturally, we would all like to follow your example and give ourselves a day out. However, we don't, because we know that our country would grind to a standstill if every worker took your attitude.

Eric Bloxham

Eric Bloxham

A concerned parent

Text 44

Lilworth Times

Lilworth *Times*

EDITORIAL

Lilworth's beauty threatened

Tradition must be respected

Does Lilworth really need a new eyesore? There's a new gym in Spender Street – and it is not right for this town.

Remember some of our previous problems?

- half-baked planning ideas
- shabby premises
- under-funded businesses
- get-rich-quick profiteers

Surely we can learn from our mistakes? Lilworthians want a town they can be proud of. You can hardly say this latest venture – Jim's Gym – meets that requirement.

So, where does that leave us?

The latest poll says that 90% of us want a fitness centre. However, that is not all. **The latest poll says that 90% of us want a PROPER fitness centre.**

The solution is clear:

- close down the inferior business in Spender Street;
- set up a working committee of professionals;
- design a facility to be proud of;
- and get it built!

Do we deserve a proper gym?
Then let's set about getting one.

Text 45

The Lilworth Weekly (1)

THE LILWORTH WEEKLY

HEALTH v. PLANNING
Health Must Come First

At last we have a gym. Let's make sure we keep it. Progress can be slow in this town. The new leisure centre in Spender Street is just what 21st century Lilworth needs.

After all, recent poll figures revealed that 90% of us had a major worry: **our fitness**. In other words, **we asked for a gym**.

Think about these places:
1. *Sunway Swim 'n Sauna*
2. *Fight the Flab Gym*
3. *Work Out Way*

Where are they now?
Exactly! They all lasted a matter of weeks, closed down because of the killjoys who moaned about land use and preservation. Of course, you have to care about the town's land, but you also have to care about the town's people.

Which is more important – a pretty building or people's health?

After all, let's think about what Jim Jewell is offering:
- experience – he used to run a gym in Workton;
- a wide range of specialised equipment – with a willingness to provide plenty of it;
- young, keen staff – they can teach professional use of the equipment;
- add-on facilities – he provides a first-rate beauty salon.

Jim Jewell is giving you a chance to get fit. Do most of you want to turn him down as well?

Recognise a good thing: *Jim's Gym* is just what this town needs.

GYM RAGE

Jim Jewell fights to save his business

By Amaljit Kraam

The recently-opened leisure club in the centre of Lilworth has already been the subject of controversy. Members have lodged complaints, many of them very minor, about the standard of the equipment available; the maintenance of the premises; and the skill of the qualified staff.

These matters reached a head on Friday morning, when a group of 12 members, led by the 65-year-old former Naval Commander, Reginald Fawcett-Major, picketed the building. The 32-year-old owner, Jim Jewell, was forced to face an angry group, demanding their money back.

There are clearly points to be made on both sides. Jewell is providing a much-needed new facility for the town, but he admits that many of his original claims had been "somewhat overstated". Nevertheless, many people feel that the protest and the talk of legal action were unnecessary. In addition, Jewell said he found many of Fawcett-Major's derogatory comments "personally insulting and uncalled for".

For the moment, Jewell has agreed to replace three broken machines; to employ another cleaner; and to have the fitness rooms repainted. In return, Fawcett-Major's threat of legal action has been suspended.

A new venture needs time for a balanced view to be taken. Fawcett-Major is known for his speedy use of the legal system: this has denied the town of amenities in the past. It will be a pity if Lilworth loses its only gym.

For and against

By Sophie Chan, *Features Editor*

Hunting is a traditional countryside sport in England. However, opposition to it is growing, as shown in the support for the *Caring Campaign.* The debate on the issue of whether or not to ban fox hunting has gone on for most of this year.

On the one side, *Caring Campaign* holds passionate views. Its members protest about:

- the number of hunts held;
- the number of animals killed.

Strong moral outrage is expressed about environmental damage and animal abuse. Some scientific sources are quoted about the fear a fox can experience, but such views are far from proven.

On the other hand, supporters of hunting speak of:

- responsible behaviour;
- no wanton cruelty permitted.

Certainly, hunts are organised carefully. Similarly, it is true that the country's fox population, already large, cannot be allowed to grow unchecked: hunt supporters argue that their sport is the most humane means of control. Equally, there is a valid point when arguing that it is country people, not city people, who are best equipped to decide on countryside matters.

It is obvious that there are points to be made on either side. Emotion is high on the subject of cruelty and animal rights, yet many farmers need to protect their livestock and reduce the number of foxes. A calm, balanced approach needs to be adopted by the Government with all viewpoints to be considered. A decision on hunting is needed before a new season begins.

Text 48

THE GAZETTE

SCHOOL TRIPS
IT'S TIME TO THINK TWICE

For too long, teachers have been taking our children out of school on the slightest pretext of educational value. In reality, the trip is all too often an easy day off work for themselves. Parents have complained in the past, but now we have heard it all: a day trip to Scotland in order to look at a stick insect!

Eileen Perkins, 52-year-old teacher of Year 5, Lilworth Primary, organised this ridiculous trip last week. *The Gazette* says it was a shameful waste of parents' money. This week's open letter from one of the parents is proof of the strength of feeling against Perkins. Hasn't anyone nearer got a stick insect they could lend her?

Did she really believe she was behaving professionally? No right thinking teacher would organise a visit that involved nine cramped hours in a coach.

Let's think about it. What do parents in this town really care about? The answers in the polls have said it often enough:

EDUCATION,
EDUCATION,
EDUCATION

The rules need to be spelt out. Before going on a school visit, teachers should ask themselves these questions:

1. **Is it necessary?**
2. **Is it cheap?**
3. **Is it worth it?**

In fact, the answers – almost always – would be:

1. **NO**
2. **NO**
3. **NO**

If the teachers don't know what to do next, *The Gazette* can tell them:

- **get on with your jobs;**
- **stay in your classrooms;**
  and
- **TEACH.**

Isn't that what we taxpayers pay you to do?

Text 49

The Lilworth Weekly (2)

THE LILWORTH WEEKLY

KEEP UP THOSE VISITS

Our children need to widen their horizons

At last we have found a teacher with initiative: Eileen Perkins, 52-year-old teacher at Lilworth Primary, ran a stupendous visit last week. She took her Year 5 class to Edinburgh Butterfly and Insect World.

Travel time and costs were kept as low as possible and parents have paid tribute to the day's success. In particular, there has been praise for Mrs Perkins' innovative approach to science teaching.

After all, just stop and think. It is not every day that you come across a teacher who is willing to move outside the comfort zone of her classroom, and travel for the sake of children's education. The easy, lazy way would be to find a local stick insect; only a true professional travels that extra mile to track down a special specimen.

The Weekly is speaking for everyone when it gives this message to teachers:

- **learn from Mrs Perkins;**
- **get your ideas moving;**
- **put the children first;**
- and... **KEEP TAKING THEM OUT.**

Text 50

The Courier

The **Courier**
First published August 9, 1828

Friday, 19 December 2003

He's everybody's Darling now

As a demonstration of people power, the campaign to 'Stop the Airport' will take some beating. Almost from that first moment 18 months ago when the bombshell was dropped on residents of Church Lawford and Stretton-on-Dunsmore and the shock waves rolled out across the rest of central Warwickshire between Leamington and Rugby, the fight to stop what was presented as Europe's largest airport was at full throttle.

Of course, there were many who just did not and could not believe it. Who in their right mind, many wondered, would dream up such a scheme? It quickly became apparent that it was not a dream but a nightmare which threatened to blight thousands of people.

Despite a number of setbacks and delays, no one and no organisation involved ever throttled back on their united opposition. It was a memorable community effort of which they can be justly proud. The big cheer from relieved MPs that greeted Transport Secretary Alistair Darling's announcement in the House of Commons on Tuesday was immediately and more loudly echoed in the leafy lanes of Warwickshire – the bad guy had suddenly joined the good guys. The MPs, and possibly Mr Darling, may have had a weather eye on the next General Election. Now, after his long-awaited statement, they and their constituents can begin to apply the air brakes and start getting back to normal.

The Leamington Spa Courier

Teaching notes and ideas

TERM 1

Note-taking and recount

1 Volcanic eruptions
Identify the text type. (A recount.) Compile a class list of key features. Stress the importance of the first sentence to orientate the reader. Ask the children to identify words which support chronological sequence (specific time references; time connectives). **T21**

Extend vocabulary and spelling: select a number of words, for example 'eruption', 'indication', 'destroyed' and 'explosions'. Ask the children for two or three words from the same root. Identify technical or specialised vocabulary (such as 'pyroclastic') and ask the children to find out the meanings. **W8**

2 The destruction of Pompeii
Compare this with the previous text. Ask the children to identify time connectives. Which sentence orientates the reader? (The first one.) **T21**

Use this text and the previous one for practice in making notes. Ask the children to prepare for a discussion on volcanoes. They need to list some key points in note form in preparation for oral contributions. **T26**

3 Outing to Bournemouth
Point out the date. How can you tell the events are set in Victorian times? (Vocabulary, attitudes and references.) Who is the likely writer? What form does the text take? What is its purpose? (The teacher has written these notes, intending to write a full recount later, or to give to her Head Teacher.) **T23**

Identify abbreviations used. Make sure the children know what they mean. What abbreviations do *they* use in note-taking? Compile a list of simple, useful abbreviations. **T27**

Link the text to history work on Victorian childhood. Ask the children to put themselves into the children's places and to write diary recounts of the day. **T24**

4 The school outing to Bournemouth
Compare this with the previous text. Consider how the notes have been used. Which part of the text orientates the reader? (The first paragraph.) Point out the formal tone and the care taken with chronological sequence. Ask the children to identify time connectives. **T21**

Ask the children to use the notes in the previous text to add a paragraph to this text. Stress the use of connectives.

5 Observation day 1
Consider the purpose and the nature of the notes. Point out the lack of formality; abbreviations; the writer's messages to herself.

Ask the children to write a set of notes for a student who was away ill. The student will be in the same school as the writer, but not in the same class. **T26**, **T27**

6 Teaching practice observation day
Set the children features to identify: connectives; chronological sequence; an introduction to orientate the reader. Explain that a recount often features a supporting illustration. Would one be useful here? (For example, a diagram of where Year 5 sat in the hall, or where the teacher stood.) Ask the children to add a helpful illustration. **T21**

Compare the formality of this text with that of the notes in the previous text. What gives the formal tone? (Word selection; some use of passive verbs; choice of punctuation; complex sentences.) Analyse some of the sentence construction. Let the children use their own writing, identifying where it could be improved by more complex sentences and a wider range of connectives. **S3**

7 The Diary of Dora Roberts – Thursday

Discuss the purpose of a diary. Consider the way the servant speaks to herself. ('I do so hope that she will bring no trouble upon herself... or upon me.')

Investigate sentence construction and the range of connectives used. Ask the children to identify the connectives. Stress the use of time connectives. **T21, S3**

8 The Diary of Dora Roberts – Friday

Revise direct and reported speech. Ask the children to re-write the passages of direct speech in reported speech. Which version is more effective? Could direct speech be added effectively in other places? **S5**

9 The Diary of Dora Roberts – Saturday

Ask the children if there are any words they do not understand. What does 'berated' mean? What is the word route of 'pronouncement'? Extend the children's vocabulary, adding words to their spelling logs. **W8**

The diary is written in a Victorian style. Which constructions or words show this? Ask the children to simplify this text (or Texts 7 or 8) to suit a modern, younger audience. **S4**

The story of Dora's Sunday visit is included in *Classworks Fiction and Poetry Year 3*, Unit 1.

10 Observation days

Allow the children to discuss these notes. Can they work out the purpose? (Cues for the University lecturer's talk to his students.) How has the lecturer helped himself? (Clear layout; organisational devices.) **T23**

Consider subjects for short talks. Ask the children to make notes, listing their cues. **T26**

Speaking and listening

Ask the children to use their notes (Text 10) to make spoken presentations. Encourage the use of appropriate vocabulary.

Discuss other purposes of note-taking.

Instructions

11 How to make a UK route-finder

Link this text with geography work. Identify key layout and language features. Are the instructions clear? Would a diagram be useful? Ask the children to supply one. **T22**

Ask the children to identify imperative forms. Give oral practice in their use. **S9**

Consider testing the instructions before writing an evaluation. **T25**

12–13 Check your personal fitness level

Consider clarity. Is there potential for confusion? Could the instructions be clearer? Ask the children to make improvements to the text to increase clarity? **T22**

Revise the term 'connective'. Point out the value of time connectives in an instructional text. Ask the children to identify examples. **S3**

Give further practice in identifying imperative verb forms. Are there examples on display in the classroom? **S9**

Point out the range of organisational devices used. How would you improve the presentation? Ask the children to evaluate Texts 12 and 13 in terms of: purpose; organisation and layout; clarity and usefulness. **T22**

Link Texts 12 and 13 to your science unit, 'Keeping healthy'. Let the children test the instructions, preparing notes for later oral feedback. **T25**

14 To save a file

How could these instructions be made clearer? (By using shorter sentences; a new line for each short instruction; time connectives; simpler language; using capitals and bold letters; including a diagram or illustration; improved layout.) **T22, S3**

Ask the children to write the next set of instructions in the computer manual – for example, **To retrieve a file** or **To create a folder**. (Link the task to your current ICT work.) Remind the children that they are writing for each other and the instructions need to be clear. **T25**

Speaking and listening

Share views on Texts 11, 12, 13. What do you find helpful when reading instructions?

Listen to one another's computer instructions (Text 14). Test them out and discuss their effectiveness.

TERM 2

Note-taking and explanation texts

15 How does the human respiratory system function?

What type of text is this? Identify passive verb forms in paragraph 1. Revise the difference between the active and the passive voice. What are the benefits here of using some verbs in the passive form? (They provide a more formal, impersonal tone.) Help the children to identify other examples of passive verb forms. **T15**

How does the passive differ from the active voice? (For example, is 'made up' rather than 'makes up'.) Model changing sentences to accommodate active verb forms, yet retaining the same meaning. Consider how words need to be re-ordered, deleted or substituted. **S8**

16 How do people breathe?

Compile a list of key features for an explanation text. Emphasise the importance of technical vocabulary and information presented in a series of steps. **T15**

Focus on sequential order. Which organisational device is helpful? (Numbered list.) Ask the children to identify words or phrases which make sequential ('as'), causal and logical connections ('so'). Consider where others could be helpful in supporting chronology. **T15**

Experiment with sentence reconstruction whilst retaining the same meaning. **S8**

17 How is sound made?

Talk about the impersonal style. How is this created? (Use of the passive voice; general references, such as 'you'.)

Which organisational devices help to make the explanation clear? (Headings and diagrams.) How does the language help? (Sequential connectives.) **T15**

Investigate the paragraph beginning, "Inside a loudspeaker..." Ask the children to rewrite it, retaining the meaning, but improving clarity. Could additional organisational devices be helpful? **S8**

18 Notes on sound changes

Discuss the text's format and purpose. Who are the notes for? (Probably the writer – because of the abbreviations and symbols used.) What is the source? (*The Usborne Internet-linked Book of Knowledge*.) Stress the care with: technical words and facts; essential spellings; names and book titles. **T20**

Ask the children to convert these personal notes into notes suitable for the rest of the class. Stress the need for clarity. **T21**

19 How are sounds changed?

Compare this with the previous text. Consider how the writer has used her notes (originally taken from Text 17). Investigate presentation; sentence and paragraph construction; organisational devices (headings, diagrams). Can this text be understood by a reader other than the writer? Point out that whereas the previous text was for personal use, this is an information text for others to read. Is the conversion of personal notes into a text for others successful? Would you alter the presentation? **T21**

Study verb forms, vocabulary and connectives. Talk about hypothetical language and refer to the sentence beginning: "For example, <u>if</u> a bee's wings..., <u>then</u> ..." Model write other sentences with this construction. **T15**

Point out the acknowledgement after the text. Revise the differences between **copying** and **adapting**. Stress the value of suitable quotes, but emphasise the need for references and accuracy. **T20**

Revise the use of commas to embed clauses within sentences. Identify examples. ('This speed, which is calculated per second, is...') Ask the children to write sentences modelled on some of these examples. **S9**

20 How do rivers shape the land?

Set questions beginning 'How' and 'Why?' Can they be answered from the text? Use scanning practice to locate information.

What do the children know already about rivers? Ask them to identify:

- what they already know about how rivers affect land;
- what they need to find out. **T16**

21 How do coasts change?

Repeat the work from Text 20 (identifying what is already known and what needs to be found out).

Ask the children to make notes on coasts and rivers, using a website (for example, www.bbc.co.uk/schools/riversandcoasts/coasts/change_coast/). Are the children familiar with this type of computer presentation? Compare with a book-based explanation, and point out differences (interaction; animation; instructions) and similarities (technical language; connectives; sequential order). **T17**

Later, let the children convert personal notes into notes suitable for the class. **T20, T21**

Think about a current area of study. Collaborate on identifying:

- what the children already know:
- what they need to find out.

Familiarise the children with information sources, including CD-ROMs and other ICT sources. Remind them to begin with notes. Allow plenty of time for planning, composing, editing and refining their texts. **T20, T22**

Speaking and listening

Use some of the children's notes from Texts 18 or 20–21. Ask other children to make oral presentations from them. Were the notes suitable?

Talk about writing 'in your own words' Do the children know how to do this? When is it acceptable to copy or quote?

Non-chronological report

22 Family life in Victorian Britain

What is the first part of this text? (Contents list.) Discuss how you – as a teacher reading this book – would use this. Ask the children how it would help you to locate information. Talk to the children about lessons that you would plan. Which pages might be helpful? Assess the benefits of a list of contents. **T16, T17**

What is the second part of the text? (Index.) How should it be used? What do the numbers refer to? why are some in bold font? (Illustrations.) What could 'g' mean? (Glossary entry.) Which references and pages would be relevant for planning a lesson? **T18**

This is half the index. Ask the children to complete it, with suitable references.

23 Family gatherings

Identify this as a non-chronological report. Stress the lack of chronology in the paragraphs – their order could easily be altered.

Consider how information can be accessed most efficiently (by using headings; scanning for information.) Give practice in locating information. How could that fact be located quickly? Which reading methods and strategies would the children use? **T17**

Investigate the punctuation used. Experiment with other choices (for example, with a colon after 'grander affair', a single sentence would be formed; the colon would signpost the meaning of the second part.) Give the children practice in using colons in this way. **S5**

24 Family outings

Point out the use of headings ('Performances'; 'Holidays'). Why are these useful? (For locating information quickly.) Ask the children to question one another on the topic. How quickly is information being located? Which reading methods are most efficient? **T17**

Can the children add another two sections to fit into this chapter on family outings? Stress the need to write in a style similar to this text.

25 Children

Refer back to Text 22. Which chapter is this text from? (Parents and Children.) Before reading the text, talk about the subject matter. Ask the children to identify:

- what they already know;
- what they want to find out.

Then let the children search for their specific information in the text. Encourage efficient methods of searching. Is scanning always adequate? Is close reading necessary for complete understanding? Compare results. **T16, T17**

Ask the children to research an area of your current history topic. Identify possible sources of information. Ask the children to write a non-chronological report. Stress the need for careful planning and editing, in order to achieve clarity, conciseness and appropriate style. **T22**

26 Index
Explain that this index is from a book entitled *Great Civilizations.* Pose the question 'How do we use Ancient Greek ideas today?' Which pages could be relevant to this question? Give the children practice in making links between words, for example, 'education' is an alternative heading when locating information about schools. **T17**

27 Philosophers and scientists
Which features make this text a non-chronological report? How well is information presented? Ask the children for oral evaluations. **T16, T19**

28 Arts and crafts in Ancient Greece
Point out the original source of this text. **T18**

Ask the children to identify some points that this text does *not* tell them about Greek arts and crafts. List the children's questions. **T16**

29 Arts and the Ancient Greeks
Return to the questions posed after the last text. Can they be answered here? What strategies are the children using to locate information?

Compare and evaluate Texts 28 and 29, recognising how information has been treated differently. Use a new source for a further comparison. **T19**

Speaking and listening
Discuss what you have already learned on one of the topics covered. What else you would like to find out? Compile questions. How can the information be located?

Set up discussion groups to edit, refine and evaluate one another's reports. (Text 25)

TERM 3

Persuasion 1

30 Jim's Gym
Hold group discussions to evaluate the persuasiveness of the leaflet. Would you be tempted to join? Why? Can you make the leaflet more effective?

Ask the children to write a leaflet to be sent to other classes, persuading them to attend a new school club. **T14, T15**

31 Spring cleaners
Investigate how this leaflet sets out to persuade. Who is being targeted? Is the leaflet persuasive? Ask the children to justify their views with references to the text.

Highlight the use of:

- rhetorical questions;
- deliberate ambiguities (overstated cleanliness claims);
- sympathetic, appealing language. **T14, T15**

Point out the need for language to suit its intended audience. Ask the children to adapt this leaflet – changing the subject, vocabulary and/or sentence structure to suit a different audience (for example, a leaflet about insurance or home security for older people; a leaflet about a play area for children). **S2**

32 Cruelty in the countryside
Consider the impact of this leaflet. What effect does the picture have? How is the reader made to feel? Ask the children to list the persuasive devices used. Is the leaflet successful? **T14**

Set up small groups. Provide each group with the same set of leaflets for evaluation, considering: clarity; persuasiveness; quality of information. Compare results. **T14**

33 The Country Dweller

Who is the target audience for this leaflet? What does the leaflet try to persuade the audience to do? Investigate persuasive devices such as rhetorical questions. Point out the effective word selection, for example the connective 'In fact' makes an opinion seem to be a fact. **T15**

Ask the children to list in note form the points made in support of fox hunting. **T16**

Compare this text with Text 32. Which is more persuasive? Why? **T14**

34 Vote Orange

Discuss the content and purpose of this leaflet. Do the children have any experience of political campaigning texts? What is the main 'selling point' the Orange Party uses? (The candidates are local people.) Investigate how information and ideas are grouped and linked. Identify persuasive devices and language. **T15**

Ask the children to work out what problems are in this constituency. What promises does the leaflet make? Ask the children to present their answers in note form. **T16**

What points could be made in favour of a candidate from outside the area? (Fresh ideas; experience of other places; wider contacts.) Ask the children to construct an argument, in note form, for such a candidate. **T19**

35 Classworks

Explain that Nelson Thornes (publisher of this book) sent this leaflet to all primary schools when they published a new Literacy series. They were very successful in selling the series. Why? Put the children into discussion groups to evaluate clarity; persuasiveness; and quality of information. Perhaps devise a scoring system. Compare and debate results.**T14**

Examine the text in detail. Who is the audience? (A teacher.) How can you tell? Which points or words will persuade the teacher to buy? **T15**

Ask the children to adapt the leaflet, so that it is aimed at a pupil. Stress that vocabulary, as well as the points made, may need to be changed in order to persuade the new audience. **S2**

36–37 Educational Visits

Explain that these are extracts from websites produced by educational locations. Who is the target audience? Which words make this apparent? Which words are likely to make a particular website successful? **T15**

Use the text for sentence level work. Focus on verbs:

- agreement tense with nouns;
- consistency of tense and subject.

Give the children practice in constructing similar sentences. **S1**

Which place is a teacher likely to choose? What makes that text persuasive? **T14**

Imagine that pupils are going to make the choice. Ask the children to adapt a section of writing appropriately. Sentence structure and vocabulary may need to change. **S2**

Consider the value of school visits. Do you think they are worthwhile, or are they a waste of school time? Ask the children to construct in note form an argument presenting a point of view. **T19**

Speaking and listening

Hold a class debate on the value of school visits.

Encourage the children to listen to and evaluate the arguments presented. Can your opinion be changed?

Persuasion 2

38 Dear Mr Jewell

Ask the children to identify, listing in note form, points that the writer makes in support of Jim's Gym. Go through them together.

Investigate language, identifying persuasive words and phrases (for example, 'clearly'; 'meaning that'; 'it stands to reason'; 'there are bound to be'; 'the truth'). **T15**

Use the text for analysis of sentence structure. Revise **clauses**. Can you identify the main clause? How are the clauses combined into one sentence? Provide further examples, so that the children can construct sentences of more than one clause. **S6**

39 Dear Sir

What type of letter is this? (Formal.) Point out the lack of punctuation in the addresses, opening and closing. Explain that modern letters are often set out in this way. Use other formal letters for comparison.

What is the letter's purpose? (Complaint.) Consider the language used. What effect does the writer want to have? (He wants to be paid attention to; to intimidate; and to get his money back.) Ask the children to justify their comments with references to the text, identifying effective words. **T12**

40 Dear Mrs Perkins... (1)

Investigate how arguments are constructed. What points are made? How is attention gained? Which language is effective? **T12**

Compile and display a list of useful persuasive devices. **T15**

Give practice in the identification of main clauses and links between clauses. **S6**

41 Dear Mrs Perkins... (2)

Analyse punctuation, particularly in complex sentences. Why are commas used there? Which connective links those two clauses? **S4**

Investigate construction of longer sentences. Point out how short sentences can be combined into a longer, complex sentence. **S6**

Ask the children to make notes on this letter. What points support Melanie's argument? How has she grouped or linked points? **T16**

Is the letter persuasive? How will Mrs Perkins react? **T12**

Set the task of writing a persuasive letter to Mrs Perkins, 'arguing the case' for visiting one of the places in Texts 36 and 37.

42 Dear Mrs Perkins... (3)

Explain that the writer is the parent of a child in Mrs Perkins' class. What is she complaining about? Ask the children to make notes on the points that Mrs Kalan makes. **T16**

Focus on the structure and persuasive devices. Have the children noticed how effectively the writer uses questions? Point out the emphasis on vocabulary linked to teaching and education; this supports the writer's complaints. **T15**

Imagine that Mrs Perkins took the class to a different place. (Look again at Texts 36 and 37.) Ask the children to write a letter of complaint related to the visit.

43 An open letter

Consider the writer's intention. (A complaint or protest printed by a newspaper.) Put the children into groups to evaluate the letter's impact. **T12**

Ask them to compile a list of effective persuasive devices. Which of the writer's words do you find persuasive? **T15**

Select a real issue relevant to the children. Ask them to draft and write letters (to you or the Head) expressing a point of view on the issue. Stress the need for persuasion. **T17**

Speaking and listening

Talk about ambiguity. Give oral examples. Discuss how deliberate ambiguity can be effective.

Listen to one another's letters (Text 43). How persuasive is the viewpoint?

Persuasion 3

44 Lilworth Times

Revise the difference between fact and opinion. Explain that this is a newspaper editorial; it expresses an opinion. What is the newspaper's opinion on the new gym? How does it try to persuade its readers to hold the same view? Investigate language, asking the children to identify persuasive words, phrases, and devices employed. **T15**

45 The Lilworth Weekly (1)

Consider this newspaper's position on the issue of the new gym. What points are made? How are they linked? Is there a connected, logical argument? What features are important in the construction of this editorial? (Issue and position stated clearly at outset; statistical data used to advantage; organisational devices.)

Explore language. Are there examples of rhetorical questions? Which words or devices are most persuasive? Are connectives used skilfully? Is opinion ever made to sound like fact? **T13, T15, S7**

Choose an issue relevant to your school or town. Discuss the issue, collecting opinions and points to be made. Ask the children to write a newspaper editorial, trying to persuade its audience of the value of a particular point of view. Stress the need for persuasive language and devices, as well as well-chosen connectives. **T18, S7**

46 Gym Rage

Study the text. Ask the children to make notes on information and points made. List them under two headings: 'FOR the gym' and 'AGAINST the gym'. **T16**

Which side of the argument does the text support? Explain that this is a balanced commentary on the issue. Analyse how the balance is achieved (calm tone; restrained, less emotive vocabulary; statements, rather than questions or exclamations; favourable references to both sides in the dispute). **T18**

Focus on the use of connectives in the commentary. Ask the children to identify examples and to investigate their purpose. (For example, 'but' introduces an opposing point.) **S7**

47 For and against

Consider how the newspaper article offers a balanced view on the issue of fox hunting. What makes it balanced? Encourage the children to support their answers with textual references.

Give practice in note-taking, asking the children to extract key points from the text. Share and display results. **T16**

Focus on connectives, investigating the links between clauses ('as shown ...'), and between sentences ('Equally, ...') and paragraphs ('On the one side, ...').

Set the task of writing an editorial, clearly supporting one side in this debate. Refer to Texts 44 and 45 for help. **T18**

48 The Gazette

Analyse how the editorial sets out and justifies a point of view. Point out the use of ambiguity. (Does one person's discontent *prove* strength of feeling? The newspaper's words give the impression that a lot of people have complained.) Identify other examples of ambiguity, half truth or bias. **T13**

Ask the children to present the editorial's argument in note form. **T16**

49 The Lilworth Weekly (2)

Identify examples of ambiguity, half truth or bias. (Vagueness about travel time and distance; no mention of complaint.) **T13**

Ask the children to plan in note form an editorial for *The Lilworth Times*, dealing with this issue of educational visits. Allow plenty of time for drafting, editing, and presenting the final version. **T18**

50 The Courier

The editorial is strongly opposed to a new airport. What reasons are given? Identify examples of emotive language, persuasive definitions, and rhetorical questions in the text ('a nightmare'; 'in their right mind'). **T15**

Investigate the use of connectives, linking clauses within sentences, and linking sentences and paragraphs. Do they improve the text? **S7**

Discuss a real environmental issue or venture in your area – raising points both for and against. Ask for a balanced, written commentary, presenting both sides of the argument. **T18**

Speaking and listening

Return to Text 50. What is opinion? What is a fact?

Listen to one another's editorials (Text 49). Focus on persuasiveness, asking the children to make oral evaluations on the effectiveness of the editorials.